12 SUPER-POISONOUS ANIMALS
YOU NEED TO KNOW

by Carol Hand

12 STORY LIBRARY

www.12StoryLibrary.com

12-Story Library is an imprint of Peterson Publishing Company and Press Room Editions.

Produced for 12-Story Library by Red Line Editorial

Photographs ©: Heiko Kiera/Shutterstock Images, cover, 1; Howard Chew/iStockphoto, 4; aquapix/Shutterstock Images, 5; Jan Bielecki/Smithsonian Institution, 6; ginosphotos/ iStockphoto, 7; Dr. Morley Read/Shutterstock Images, 8, 9; Yair Goldstof, 10; Krofoto/ Shutterstock Images, 13; Tim Laman/National Geographic Creative, 15; oxime/iStockphoto, 16; Susan Schmitz/Shutterstock Images, 17; skynavin/iStockphoto, 18; Benzine/ Shutterstock Images, 19; kikkerdirk/iStockphoto, 20, 28; Artur Janichev/Shutterstock Images, 21; FtLaudGirl/iStockphoto, 22; Moize Nicolas/Shutterstock Images, 23, 29; hairballusa/iStockphoto, 24; Sphinx Wang/Shutterstock Images, 25; warmer/iStockphoto, 26; GreyCarnation/iStockphoto, 27

ISBN
978-1-63235-140-1 (hardcover)
978-1-63235-182-1 (paperback)
978-1-62143-234-0 (hosted ebook)

Library of Congress Control Number: 2015934278

Printed in the United States of America
Mankato, MN
June, 2015

Go beyond the book. Get free, up-to-date content on this topic at 12StoryLibrary.com.

TABLE OF CONTENTS

BLUE-RINGED OCTOPUSES: TINY BUT DEADLY

There are 10 kinds of blue-ringed octopuses and all are tiny. The most common has a body approximately two inches (5.1 cm) across. That is the size of a golf ball. When alarmed, bright blue rings appear around its arms. The tiny octopus is beautiful, but its bite can kill. One blue-ringed octopus contains enough venom to kill 26 adult humans. The venom can kill a person within minutes of being bit.

The blue-ringed octopus lives in tide pools and coral reefs along coasts in the Pacific and Indian Oceans. Many live on Australia's Great Barrier Reef. The octopus uses its venom to defend against predators. They bite if they feel threatened or if they are stepped on. Blue-ringed octopuses inject venom that paralyzes, or makes the person or animal unable to move. This can cause death because breathing stops. Humans can survive a blue-ringed octopus bite if doctors use machines to help them breathe until the venom is gone.

The blue-ringed octopus releases a second toxin to hunt small crabs for food. Both toxins are released in the

The blue-ringed octopus's arms are approximately four inches (10 cm) long.

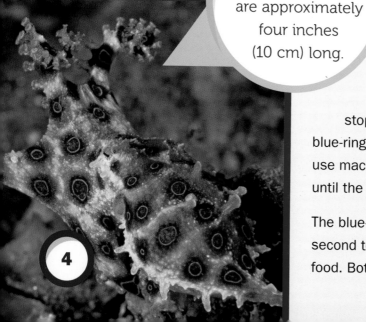

2

Number of venom glands used by a blue-ringed octopus.

- Blue rings form on blue-ringed octopuses arms when they are alarmed.
- They bite when threatened.
- They inject venom that can paralyze and kill.
- Blue-ringed octopuses live on Australia's Great Barrier Reef.

octopuses' saliva. No one knows for sure how they kill their food. They may spit the toxin into the water, or bite the crabs.

THINK ABOUT IT

Explain the difference between poison, toxins, and venom. Describe how a substance can fit in more than one of these groups. Identify which group or groups the blue-ringed octopus produces.

The venom in blue-ringed octopuses is stronger than any found in land animals.

POISONS, TOXINS, AND VENOMS

Blue-ringed octopuses are one of many animals that can be deadly. A poison is any chemical that can cause illness or death of an organism. A toxin is a poison produced by a plant or animal. Animals and people may ingest toxins through food or drink. Toxins may also enter through the skin. Venom is a toxin that enters the body through a bite or sting, such as an octopus bite or bee sting.

BOX JELLYFISH KILL WITH STINGING TENTACLES

Box jellyfish are also called box jellies or sea wasps. Their tentacles have stinging cells that contain powerful venom. They use the venom to stun their prey, such as shrimp or fish. The box jellies' venom is one of the most deadly toxins in the world. When a person is stung, the venom attacks the heart, nervous system, and skin cells.

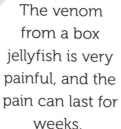

The venom from a box jellyfish is very painful, and the pain can last for weeks.

Most people stung by box jellies do not die. But being stung by multiple tentacles can cause death. A person can die within three minutes after a box jelly sting. The person may drown or die of heart failure. Box jellies have killed approximately 100 people in the past 100 years.

Box jellies live off the coast of northern Australia and throughout the tropical Indian and Pacific Oceans. Their bodies are cube-shaped. They are approximately the size of a human head. Fifteen tentacles grow

from each corner of the body. Each tentacle can be up to 10 feet (3 m) long.

Unlike most jellies, box jellyfish do not drift through the ocean. They swim by jetting water out the back of their bodies. They swim up to approximately 4.6 miles (7.4 km) per hour.

Box jellies are transparent and are hard to see in the water.

BRAZILIAN WANDERING SPIDERS BITE IN SELF-DEFENSE

People call the Brazilian wandering spider the world's most venomous spider. But two things determine how deadly an animal is. One is how much venom it injects. The other is how big of an animal it bites. The same amount of spider venom might kill a mouse, but not a human.

Some bites from this spider are not dangerous to people. Others are serious and require quick treatment.

Bites cause pain and swelling. Too much venom paralyzes the person and stops breathing. But of 7,000 known bites by Brazilian wandering spiders, only 10 people have died.

Brazilian wandering spiders are large spiders. Their bodies are up to two inches (5.1 cm) long, and their legs may be

The venom from a Brazilian wandering spider bite attacks muscles.

six inches (15 cm) long. Wandering spiders travel over the forest floor at night, hunting insects, other spiders, and small mice or frogs.

Brazilian wandering spiders look scary. Many people consider them aggressive, or likely to attack. As a warning, the spiders raise their first two pairs of legs and sway from side to side. Then they bite in self-defense.

Wandering spiders do not build webs.

8

Number of species of Brazilian wandering spiders.

- The Brazilian wandering spider is the world's most venomous spider.
- Its bites are painful, but rarely kill.
- These large spiders do not build webs, but hunt on the forest floor.
- They look aggressive but bite only in self-defense.

THE DEADLY BANANA SPIDER

Brazilian wandering spiders sometimes hitch rides in boxes of bananas. In 2014, a man in Great Britain bought bananas from a local shop. The box contained a nest with hundreds of young Brazilian wandering spiders, which got loose in his home. He had to leave until they were removed.

DEATHSTALKER SCORPIONS KILL WITH THEIR TAILS

The deathstalker scorpion has venom in its tail. It hunts by hiding under rocks and waiting. The scorpion grabs a cricket with its pincers and stings it with its tail.

Deathstalkers are yellow or orange in color.

25

Number of years a deathstalker scorpion can live.

- The deathstalker scorpion has venom in its tail.
- The sting is painful, but does not kill most adults.
- Deathstalkers live in North Africa and Southeast Asia.
- Their venom is used in surgery and to treat brain tumors.

DEATHSTALKERS SAVE LIVES

Doctors have discovered that deathstalker venom can save lives. They use it to stop brain tumors from growing. In rare cases, doctors use it in surgery. The venom causes paralysis. A small dose of venom keeps the patient from moving during the operation.

Its pincers are not very powerful, so it must sting quickly. The scorpion paralyzes or kills the cricket.

The deathstalker scorpion hunts mostly at night. Deathstalkers are excellent predators, but they are prey, too. Other larger animals eat deathstalkers. These include other kinds of scorpions, large centipedes, and bats. Deathstalker venom does not hurt bats, but no one understands why.

The deathstalker scorpion sometimes stings people. It can kill children and older adults. It affects the heart and causes the lungs to fill with fluid. The person cannot breathe and may die. It usually does not kill healthy adults. But its sting is very painful.

Females are approximately four inches (10 cm) long and males are approximately three inches (7.6 cm). The scorpion lives in North Africa and Southeast Asia. It prefers dry climates, but not sand dunes.

FAINT-BANDED SEA SNAKES ARE TIMID

The faint-banded sea snake is also called Belcher's sea snake. Its venom is highly toxic. One milligram of its venom is enough to kill 1,000 people. But Belcher's sea snakes are timid and rarely kill people. They only bite when they are threatened.

25
Percent of faint-banded sea snake bites that contain venom.

- One milligram of faint-banded sea snake venom can kill 1,000 people.
- They do not always release venom.
- Sea snakes live around islands in the Indian Ocean and the Gulf of Thailand.
- Sea snakes live entirely in the ocean and travel in huge swarms.

Usually they bite fishermen who pull them up in fishing nets.

A sea snake's bite is not very painful. Sometimes people do not notice it. Only one in four bites contain venom. This is because sea snakes do not release venom with every bite. But a bite containing venom can kill within 30 minutes. The person loses feeling and the body becomes paralyzed. If the loss of movement reaches the lungs, the person dies of suffocation.

Sea snakes live in the Indian Ocean and the Gulf of Thailand. Sea snakes live their entire lives in the ocean. They are air breathers, but sleep under water. They can hold their breath for up to eight hours. Sea snakes travel in huge swarms. The largest known swarm contained 1 million snakes and stretched for 0.6 miles (1 km).

Sea snakes range from 1.6 to 3.3 feet (0.48 to 1 m) in length.

HOODED PITOHUIS ARE TOXIC TO TOUCH

The hooded pitohui lives only in tropical rain forests on the Pacific island of New Guinea. Scientists discovered this bird was toxic in 1989. When it scratched them, the scratched area became numb and irritated. Sucking on the scratch made their lips tingle and burn. New Guinea indigenous people eat pitohuis. But first, they rub them in charcoal to remove the toxin.

The hooded pitohui has toxin in its feathers and skin. It is a neurotoxin, which attacks the nervous system. Touching the pitohui causes only minor numbness and tingling, because it has very little toxin. Larger amounts would cause paralysis and death. The toxin protects hooded pitohuis from parasites, such as lice. Pitohuis are brightly colored and they smell and taste bad. These things warn possible predators, such as snakes, to stay away.

Pitohuis get toxin from the beetles they eat. This means not all birds have the same amount of toxin. Most of the toxin settles in their skin and in the breast, belly, and leg feathers. Nestlings do not have the toxin. Adult birds may transfer it from their feathers to the young's feathers.

1989
Year scientists discovered the hooded pitohui was toxic.

- Hooded pitohuis live in New Guinea rain forests.
- They get neurotoxins in their skin and feathers from the beetles they eat.
- The small amount of toxin only causes numbness and tingling.
- The birds' bright colors, bad smell, and bad taste warn away predators.

The toxin in pitohuis protects them from most predators.

7

INLAND TAIPANS ARE FIERCE AND DEADLY

The inland taipan has the most toxic venom of any snake. It lives only in one part of Australia, around the border where Queensland and the Northern Territory meet. People there call it the "fierce snake." The taipan feeds mostly on rats. It slows them down by several very fast, accurate strikes. The strikes cause the taipan's fangs to send venom deep into the rat. The venom acts quickly, so the rat has no time to fight back before it dies.

There is enough venom in one bite of an inland taipan to kill 100 adult humans. But they rarely bite people, partly because few people live in their habitat.

Inland taipans vary in color from light brown to black. They become darker in winter.

16

Average number of eggs a female inland taipan lays.

- The inland taipan has the most toxic snake venom in the world.
- The taipan feeds mostly on rats, which it kills with several rapid strikes.
- Humans are seldom bitten, but they can be saved by antivenom.
- Taipans detect prey by sensing movement with their eyes and odor with their tongues.

People who are bitten survive because they receive taipan antivenom. This is a chemical used to treat someone poisoned by venom. There are special types of antivenom for different animal venoms.

Inland taipans are usually around 6.5 feet (2 m) long, but can grow up to 8.8 feet (2.7 m) long. Taipans detect prey by sensing movement with their keen eyesight. They also

THINK ABOUT IT

There are several reasons an animal might need to use a toxin or venom. List a few examples of animals that use these chemicals to capture food and to defend themselves or their young.

flick their tongues out to taste the prey's odor in the air.

Inland taipans live in hot and dry climates.

KING COBRAS HISS BEFORE THEY STRIKE

The king cobra is not the world's most venomous snake. But it is still very poisonous. It is also big and scary. A king cobra averages 13 feet (4 m) in length, but can reach up to 18 feet (5.5 m) long.

That is as long as three six-foot (1.8-m) men lying end to end. The cobra is shy. But when threatened, it raises part of its body straight off the ground.

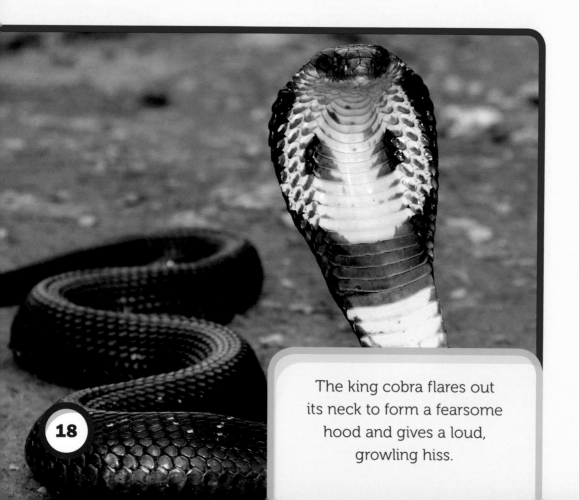

The king cobra flares out its neck to form a fearsome hood and gives a loud, growling hiss.

The cobra's venom is less toxic than the inland taipan's. But because of its large size, the venom in a single bite can kill 20 men or one elephant. The cobra injects venom through its hollow fangs. The venom is a neurotoxin. It will stop a person's breathing and heartbeat.

Cobras eat many small animals. They prefer mice, rats, ground squirrels, or rabbits. They live in the rain forests or on the plains of India, southern China, and Southeast Asia.

To survive a bite from a king cobra, a victim must receive cobra antivenom.

CHARMING A COBRA

A snake charmer in Southeast Asia sits in front of a cobra and "charms" it by playing a gourd flute. But the cobra is not attracted by the music. Cobras are deaf. Instead of hearing, they sense vibrations in the ground. The cobra sways to the movement of the flute, rather than the sound.

20
Average number of years a wild king cobra lives.

- The king cobra lifts one-third of its body, spreads its hood, and hisses when threatened.
- One bite of its venom can kill 20 men or one elephant.
- The cobra's venom is a neurotoxin.

POISON DART FROGS ARE BRIGHT AND TOXIC

Visitors to Central or South American rain forests will see brilliant spots of color near the forest floor. These bright spots are poison dart frogs. There are more than 175 kinds. Most are tiny enough to fit in a bottle cap. Their colors vary from bright blue to yellow to copper to red. Many have black stripes or zigzags.

Their poison may cause swelling, nausea, and paralysis. But they taste terrible. A careless predator who eats one will not try another. Only one animal—a small snake—is resistant to the dart frogs' poison, and eats them. The snake will not become sick unless the toxin is very strong.

Three kinds of poison dart frogs are dangerous to humans. The most poisonous is the golden poison dart frog. Its two-inch (5.1-cm) body contains enough poison to kill 10 adult humans. The poison is in the frog's skin. Scientists are not sure where dart frogs get their poison. They think it is absorbed from insect prey such as ants, termites, and beetles.

The bright colors warn possible predators that poison dart frogs are toxic.

30

Number of eggs a female poison dart frog lays.

- Poison dart frogs live in Central and South American rain forests.
- They are brightly colored and very tiny.
- A few species have deadly poisons in their skin.
- Colombia's Choco people coat their blowgun darts in poison dart frog venom.

POISON DARTS FOR BLOWGUNS

The Choco people of Colombia coat the tips of their blowgun darts with poison from the golden poison dart frog. One two-inch (5.1-cm) frog contains enough poison to coat 30 to 50 darts.

Most poison dart frogs are not deadly.

PUFFER FISH ARE DEADLY TREATS

Puffer fish, or blowfish, are slow, clumsy swimmers. To protect themselves, they ingest large amounts of water. They swell up into a ball three times their normal size. Their skin and spines contain a dangerous neurotoxin. This makes them taste bad and can kill anything that eats them. It is the same toxin found in the blue-ringed octopus. The puffer fish is the second-most toxic animal in the world, after the golden poison dart frog.

The toxin in one puffer fish can kill 30 adult humans. There is no known antidote. The toxin makes a person's mouth feel numb and tingly. They become paralyzed and stop breathing. If untreated, they die. Doctors try to

Humans and other animals must avoid a puffer fish's skin and spines.

FUGU

In Japan, the puffer fish is called "fugu." Some people consider it a treat. They pay high prices to eat it in restaurants. Trained chefs prepare fugu. They know how to cut it to avoid the toxin. Still, some people die from puffer fish poisoning every year.

make the person throw up to get rid of the poison.

Most puffer fish live in tropical and subtropical oceans.

There are more than 120 different kinds of puffer fish. They range in size from one inch (2.5 cm) to more than two feet (0.61 m) long. Not all puffer fish are poisonous. They eat algae, clams, and shellfish. Scientists think they make their toxin from bacteria in their food.

1,200

Number of times stronger than cyanide the puffer fish neurotoxin is.

- Puffer fish protect themselves by swelling into a ball.
- Puffer fish skin and spines contain a deadly neurotoxin.
- Not all 120 kinds of puffer fish are poisonous.
- Some people eat specially prepared puffer fish, called fugu.

THINK ABOUT IT

Some poisonous animals such as the puffer fish blend in because their colors match their environments. Think about why poisonous animals might have different color patterns. Consider which type of color pattern would best help them survive, and why.

SEA ANEMONES SIT STILL AND KILL

Sea anemones are related to corals and jellyfish. They live attached to rocks near ocean shores and come in all colors. A ring of tentacles surrounds their central mouths. There are more than 1,000 species of sea anemones.

When a fish swims by, its movement triggers stinging cells on the sea anemone's tentacles. The cells release tiny harpoon-like barbs on long threads. Each barb is filled with neurotoxin, which paralyzes the prey. The anemone uses the threads to pull the prey into its mouth.

One type of anemone has the scientific name *Palythoa toxica*. It has a deadly toxin called palytoxin. *Palythoa* was discovered in Hawaii but also lives in Japan and the Bahamas. No one is sure where palytoxin comes from. Some people think the tiny algae living inside anemones make it. As more algae build up in an anemone, it becomes more toxic.

Sea anemones range in size from 0.5 inch (1.3 cm) to 6 feet (1.8 m) across.

Sea anemones live in colonies of varying sizes.

A tiny dose of palytoxin kills a mouse in minutes. A barely visible amount can kill an adult human. It is most toxic when injected and much less toxic when taken in through the skin. It causes muscle weakness and bleeding. It affects the heart. The toxin lowers blood pressure and slows blood flow to different parts of the body. This can lead to death. But few people die, because most receive poison through the skin, not by injection.

1

Length, in inches (2.5 cm), of an individual *Palythoa* anemone.

- Anemones attach to rocks and have tentacles with stinging cells.
- The *Palythoa* anemone contains a toxin called palytoxin.
- Palytoxin affects the heart and limits blood flow to organs.
- Touching a *Palythoa* anemone is dangerous but unlikely to cause death.

12

SLOW LORISES IMITATE COBRAS

Some mammals can be deadly because they are fierce predators with claws and sharp teeth. Few people fear mammals for their poisons. But one mammal is different. The slow loris is a primate. Slow lorises are cute and appear harmless. Slow lorises move slowly and sleep much of the time. They are solitary animals. They spend most of their time alone.

When threatened, the slow loris becomes defensive. It hisses and backs up, clasping its hands on top of its head. In this position, with its black face markings, it looks similar to a striking cobra. It even moves from side to side, like a snake. But this pose is only part of the slow loris's defense.

Slow lorises live in the forests of Southeast Asia and Indonesia.

Slow lorises can freeze in one position for hours, watching for prey.

With its arms up, it can quickly suck venom from its armpits. Then, it bites its attacker. The bite is poisonous enough to kill a person. Lorises also mix their venom with saliva and lick their fur to discourage predators. They lick their babies' fur to protect them from predators too.

Slow lorises live in trees and are active at night. Their grip on tree branches is very strong. They eat fruits, insects, and small prey such as eggs, lizards, and birds. They may hang upside down by their feet and eat with both hands.

90
Percent of time a slow loris spends alone.

- The slow loris lives in forests of Southeast Asia and Indonesia.
- Its defensive pose makes it look similar to a cobra.
- Its armpits contain venom, which it sucks out and injects by biting.
- Slow lorises lick themselves and their babies with venom for protection.

FACT SHEET

- Animals adapt in many ways to capture food and protect themselves. One way they adapt is by producing toxins. Plants or animals produce poisons called toxins. A venom is a toxin injected by a bite or sting. Other toxins are ingested or rubbed on the skin.

- Many poisonous animals live in the oceans. The blue-ringed octopus and the box jellyfish live in the tropical Pacific and Indian Oceans. The blue-ringed octopus produces a strong venom for protection and a weaker one to stun prey. Box jellies have tentacles with stinging cells. The cells release a painful and sometimes deadly toxin that attacks the skin, heart, and nervous system.

- Sometimes animals use toxins for protection if they are slow or otherwise unable to get away from predators. The puffer fish and slow loris are both slow-moving animals. The *Palythoa* anemone does not move. It lives attached to the ocean floor. It captures food by moving its tentacles and stunning prey with the toxin in cells on the tentacles. But it cannot avoid predators. It uses its toxin-filled tentacles to attack predators as well as prey.

- Antivenom can cure people who have received venomous bites. Antivenom is made from the venom of the animal causing the bite. It breaks down the venom and removes it from the body. Antivenom is often used to cure people from the bites of poisonous snakes, such as cobras. Most venoms are neurotoxins, which act very quickly. This means the person must receive the antivenom almost immediately to survive.

GLOSSARY

antidote
A chemical given to counteract a poison, so the poison does not cause harm.

antivenom
A chemical used to treat someone poisoned by a bite containing venom.

ingest
Take a chemical into the body through food or drink.

inject
Take a chemical into the body through a bite or sting.

nervous system
The system that controls the brain, spinal cord, and nerves.

neurotoxin
A toxin that attacks the nervous system, causing numbness and tingling, and sometimes paralysis and death.

paralysis
Loss of the body's ability to move caused by illness, poison, or injury.

pincer
Front claw of a lobster, crab, or scorpion.

poison
Any chemical that causes illness or death in an animal.

tentacle
A long, thin, flexible arm on an animal used for grasping, stinging, moving, or sensing.

toxin
A poisonous chemical produced by a plant or animal.

venom
A poisonous chemical injected, or taken into the body, by a bite or sting.

FOR MORE INFORMATION

Books

Bredeson, Carmen. *Poison Dart Frogs Up Close*. Berkeley Heights, NJ: Enslow Elementary, 2009.

Riehecky, Janet. *Poisons and Venom: Animal Weapons and Defenses*. Mankato, MN: Capstone Press, 2012.

Simon, Seymour. *Poisonous Snakes*. Mineola, NY: Dover Publications, 2012.

Singer, Marilyn. *Venom*. Plain City, OH: Darby Creek Publishing, 2007.

Websites

National Geographic: Toxic and Stinging Sea Creatures
ocean.nationalgeographic.com/ocean/photos/toxic-sea-creatures

National Zoo: Poison Dart Frogs
nationalzoo.si.edu/animals/amazonia/facts/fact-poisondartfrog.cfm

Texas Parks and Wildlife: Poisonous Snakes
www.tpwd.texas.gov/kids/wild_things/wildlife/snakes.phtml

INDEX

About the Author

Carol Hand grew up on a farm and has always had pets. She has a PhD in zoology with a specialty in ecology. She writes freelance science books—whenever possible about animals and the environment. Currently, she shares her home with four cats, all rescues and, fortunately, not poisonous.

READ MORE FROM 12-STORY LIBRARY

Every 12-Story Library book is available in many formats, including Amazon Kindle and Apple iBooks. For more information, visit your device's store or 12StoryLibrary.com.